Adopting Ginger

Based on a true story about a shelter dog and the loving family who adopted her

Story by Linda Griffin, MS
Illustrations by Iliana Weinbaum

Griffinbooks.net

Cover photo by David Golod

ISBN: 147939355X
ISBN 13: 9781479393558

Library of Congress Control Number: 2012918187
CreateSpace, North Charleston, South Carolina

This book is dedicated to the extraordinary, devoted, hard-working staff and volunteers of the SPCA of Westchester in Briarcliff Manor, New York.

Thank you to Dr. Raymond Hayes, DVM
for his devotion to the animals in his care.

"Hurry up, hurry up!" I say excitedly.

It's hard for me to sit still and eat my breakfast. Today is the day we are going to the animal shelter to look for a dog! Mom, Dad, my brother, Aiden, and I have talked about adopting a dog for a year. We know having a dog is a big responsibility, but Aiden and I have agreed to take turns feeding, brushing, and walking the dog. We're not happy about picking up the poop, but we know that's part of the job.

"Remember," Mom says with a serious look on her face. "You'll have to walk the dog in the pouring rain and freezing cold."

"You'll have to take care of the dog before you meet your friends and before you use the computer," Dad reminds us.

"We know," Aiden and I say together.

Our car turns into the shelter and we see a sign that says: **Meet Your New Best Friend Today,** and we hear barking.

"I can't wait!" I shout.

"Emma," Dad says, smiling. "We'll be there in just a minute."

Once inside the gate, the car stops and I'm out the door in a flash. Aiden is right behind me. The dogs are loud and their excitement grows the closer we get to the kennels. Aiden and I stop to look at the first dogs.

"Let's get one of these!" I yell.

"They are much too large for our small house," Mom says.

We spot several medium-sized dogs in the next row of kennels. The first dog, Max, is almost all black with pointy ears and a slender body. He approaches us slowly. Max has gentle eyes and shiny, silky fur.

I whisper, not wanting to scare him, "I want to take Max home."

"Let's see other dogs before we make a decision," Dad says.

5

The second dog, Buster, is the color of chocolate ice cream. Buster's body is low to the ground and he has big floppy ears. Buster seems to be smiling as he walks over to greet us.

"I want to take Buster home," Aiden says, excitedly.

"Can we take home two dogs?" I ask.

"No!" Mom and Dad say at the same time. They both start to laugh.

"We would love to take home *all* the dogs," Dad says, "but we just don't have the room. Besides, we need to leave some dogs for other families."

As the third dog walks over to us, her entire behind sways back and forth. Her tail wags like a windshield wiper on high speed. She presses her body against the kennel door and tries to get as close to us as possible. I squeeze my hand through the bars even though there is a sign that says: **Do not put your hand in the kennel.** Ginger's wet tongue licks each finger of my hand, and when she's finished I pet her soft ears.

"Ginger has a wiggly, jiggly behind," Dad laughs.

"Ginger is a sweet potato," Mom says.

"I want to take the wiggly, jiggly sweet potato home!" I shout.

We're told that Ginger arrived a week ago from an overcrowded shelter in South Carolina and made the twelve-hour bus trip to Westchester County, New York, hoping to find her forever home.

"Before we decide on any dog we need to know if it will get along with our cat, Natasha," Mom reminds us.

An SPCA staff member takes Ginger to the cat kennels and brings her to the cage of their most aggressive cat. If Ginger growls and charges the cat, we won't get to take Ginger home.

The cat hisses and swipes at Ginger through the bars. Aiden and I jump back and bump into each other. Ginger could care less. She turns her head and walks away. *Yay for Ginger!*

Mom, Dad, Aiden, and I talk to Ginger and decide to take her for a walk around the shelter's property. Ginger leans into my leg and makes it impossible to walk.

Instead of walking, we sit down on a bench and take turns petting her short brown and black fur. Ginger lifts her head and looks right into my eyes as if to say, *Please, please take me home.*

13

The shelter's trainer says, "Ginger is a sweet dog, but she is fearful and needs to build confidence."

"She's scared and needs help to feel safe and happy," Dad says.

After a family discussion, we decide that Ginger is coming home with us. We love her gentle nature and her cute, funny face.

We wait nervously outside while Mom and Dad fill out the necessary paperwork so we can take Ginger home. It seems to take forever before we are in the car. Ginger cuddles with Aiden and me in the backseat as Dad drives the short distance to our home. I'm so happy that I can't stop smiling.

We arrive home and soon find out just how afraid Ginger is. Ginger refuses to eat. She won't even take a treat from us.

"Is Ginger sick?" I ask.

"Is Ginger going to die like our turtle did?" Aiden asks.

Dad doesn't answer. He rushes to the phone to call our veterinarian. My heart is racing as we wait to hear if Ginger will be OK.

Dad repeats what the vet tells him. "It is not unusual for a shelter dog to refuse food for a few days. As long as Ginger is drinking water, she'll be fine."

"Thank goodness," I say as I jump up and down.

Relieved, we put on Ginger's leash and go outside. Our house is on the bottom of a hill and the street is above. Ginger won't walk up the steep steps from our house to the street. She weighs forty pounds, but Dad carries her up the driveway to the road. Ginger walks a few steps then sits down, still like a statue. Dad encourages her to walk a few more steps, but Ginger bolts into the bushes and hides. Since she won't respond to treats, it takes a long time, and a lot of patience, to get her to come out.

Just as Ginger comes out of her hiding place a garbage truck rumbles and squeals down the street. Ginger bolts down the driveway for the safety of our house. She yanks with all her might, pulling so hard on the leash that Dad almost falls over.

Safely inside, Ginger walks by our cat Natasha. The cat stares at Ginger and then runs to hide in the bedroom. Ginger pays no attention to Natasha. She goes to her new soft, fluffy bed, plops herself down, and looks at us as if to say, *Ah, this is much better.*

We all sit down for a quick lunch. Ginger nuzzles each of us, stretches out on the floor near the kitchen table, and watches us eat.

Mom looks at Dad and says, "Our vacation is over at the end of this week. Emma and Aiden won't be able to walk Ginger if things continue as they are. When will Ginger start eating?"

"When will Ginger walk up the steps?" Dad asks.

"When will Ginger stop hiding?" Mom asks in return.

Aiden has a worried look on his face.

I stare at my peanut butter sandwich and start to cry. "You're *not* going to bring her back to the shelter," I say as I sob.

"Ginger is now a member of our family," Dad says. "She's our responsibility and we're going to do whatever it takes to help her feel better."

"Think how scary this must be for her," Mom says. "Ginger was in one shelter and shipped a long distance to another. Now she finds herself in yet *another* place with strange people. Let's make a plan to help build Ginger's self-confidence."

We immediately start to work to help Ginger feel less afraid.

23

Aiden and I take turns talking softly to Ginger, rubbing behind her ears, and stroking her belly. We keep Ginger with us as we go about our day.

The attention we give Ginger pays off, because by day three, Ginger is eating a little and we are able to use treats to encourage her to walk up the stairs. Dad walks up three steps, shows Ginger a treat, and pulls gently on the leash. Ginger walks up three steps and Dad gives Ginger a big hug. When Ginger refuses to take a treat and walk any further, Dad takes her back to the house. Mom tries again later, and this time Ginger walks up *six* steps.

Every day, Ginger manages to walk up a few more steps, and each time we shower Ginger with hugs and kisses.

Next we work on Ginger's fear of the driveway.

Aiden and I line the driveway with treats, placing them a few feet apart. I walk Ginger halfway up the driveway and watch as she proudly eats the treats and gets hugs as she overcomes her fear.

Aiden holds the leash for the last part of the driveway. When Ginger reaches the top, Aiden says, "Good girl!" and Ginger gives us a doggy-smile.

By the end of the week, Ginger is eating all of her food, running up the steps, racing up the driveway, and walking down the block. She only hides when she hears a loud or strange noise.

By the end of the month, Ginger walks down the block like she owns it, is frightened only by the big, noisy garbage truck, and knows her two nicknames.

I say, "Ginger Pops, come!"

Aiden says, "Hey, Gingerino!" and Ginger comes running.

Ginger follows Aiden and me around the house. When we watch TV, she curls up next to us. At bedtime, she sleeps with me. She starts out at the foot of the bed, but by early morning, her head is next to mine on the pillow. Sometimes she snores softly and wakes me up.

Sometimes Ginger and our cat Natasha cuddle on the sofa. They've become good friends.

Sometimes we come home to find that Ginger has collected things we've left on the floor and has piled them up in her bed: Aiden's socks, my towel, Dad's hat, and one of Mom's slippers have all found their way to Ginger's bed. I guess she likes the house to be neat.

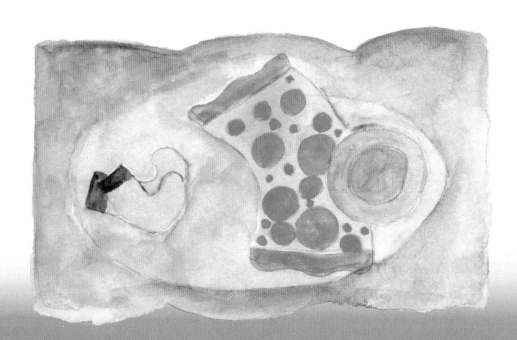

Whenever one of us comes home, we get what my family calls the "Ginger Wag"—a wiggly, jiggly behind and a fast moving tail. I love coming home to Ginger's welcome.

"Wouldn't it be nice," Mom says, "if we always greeted each another in a way that showed how happy we were to see one another?"

The next day, Mom goes out to do some errands. When she comes home, we have a surprise for her. As soon as we hear Mom's car pull in the driveway, Dad, Aiden, Ginger, and I line up by the front door. When Mom opens the door, Ginger immediately starts her Ginger Wag. We join in with our own versions of wiggly, jiggly behinds.

Mom starts laughing, gives each of us a hug, and says, "Ginger, look at the joy you have brought to our house. We love you!"

Discussion Questions

- What could be some of the reasons Ginger wound up in a shelter?
- Do you think Emma's family was ready to adopt a dog? Why or why not?
- Would you have taken Ginger home, knowing she was fearful?
- The family was looking for a sweet, medium-sized dog that got along with cats. What are some other things to consider before choosing a dog?
- Why was the cat an important part of the story?
- At one point, Emma thought her parents might return Ginger to the shelter. What did you think was going to happen when the family found out just how frightened Ginger was?
- Besides the cost of food and Ginger's new fluffy bed, what other expenses must the family consider before adopting a dog?
- What can you do to support your local animal shelter?

1710081R00019

Made in the USA
San Bernardino, CA
20 January 2013